CONTENTS

The Convent of Santo Domingo
and the Dominican Order

Together with the Franciscans and the Augustinians, the Dominicans belong to the regular clergy, to the orders known as
mendicants. These orders were formed during the Middle Ages
based on rules laid down by their founders. The history of the
Dominicans goes back to the 13th century (1215) when
Domingo de Guzmán gathered a together group of preachers
in the south of France and founded an order that was sanc-
tioned by Pope Innocent III. From the beginning they were
missionaries and their evangelizing efforts spread to north-
ern Europe, Russia, North Africa and the Middle East.

SANTO DOMINGO

CONVENT AND CHURCH

MUSEUM OF OAXACAN CULTURES

Cover:
Facade of the Convent of Santo Domingo,
Oaxaca.
Photograpy: G. Dagli Orti

Text: Laura Piñeirua

Translation by: David B. Castledine

Photographs:
G. Dagli Orti
Monclem Archives

◖ CONACULTA • INAH ❀
Reproducción autorizada por el
Instituto Nacional de Antropología e Historia

© 2002 by Monclem Ediciones, S.A. de C.V.
Leibnitz 31, Col. Anzures 11590 - México, D.F.
monclem@monclem.com
Tel.: 52 55 47 67

Printed in Mexico
Impreso en México
ISBN 970-9019-16-3

Founded in the 16th century, the Convent of Santo Domingo de Guzmán is one of the finest examples of colonial architecture. This photograph shows the church and convent.

They arrived in America in the 16th century in answer to a call from Hernán Cortés, who pressed for the conversion of Indians' idolatrous souls to Christianity. The first Dominican friars, who set sail in early 1526, came from the provinces of Castile and Andalusia and were given accommodation by the Franciscans until they established their own church and convent to later, after a series of unforeseen circumstances and difficulties, devote themselves to the task of evangelization. The territory they occupied in colonial times was what comprises the modern states of Morelos, Tlaxcala, the bishopric of Oaxaca, part of Campeche, Chiapas and Yucatán. Here they founded convents in strategic points to convert the Indians. Built between the 16th and 17th centuries, the convent of Santo

Upper part of the facade of the convent. *It finishes in a depiction of the three theological virtues. On the left, Faith is holding a chalice and a cross, Hope carries a balance, and beneath the feet of Charity is the emblem of the Dominican order.*

Domingo de Guzmán is without a doubt one of the most beautiful examples of Dominican architecture. It is not known who was in charge of construction, but it is thought that a Dominican friar was made responsible for drawing up the plans. There were various difficulties to be faced during the building of it, mainly economic, which were finally overcome so that the work could be finished. It functioned as a convent from 1608 to 1857, during which time it was the seat of the province of San Pedro Mártir; from the Independence it was used as barracks and as a result of the Reform Laws was abandoned by the Dominicans to be occupied by the army. From 1866 to 1902 it was closed for worship, looted and wrecked. Several of the altarpieces were lost, together with other works. In 1938 it was given back to the clergy, when the administration of the church was returned, although half of the convent was ceded to Benito Juárez University.

In 1972, the Regional Museum of Oaxaca was created under the auspices of the National Institute of Anthropology and History (INAH), so that by 1993 the building was devoted to cultural ends. Shortly afterward, it was decided to restore and enlarge it and to add a botanical garden, thus it was preserved at the same time as its functions were channeled toward the diffusion and conservation of Oaxacan culture. In 2001 it won the Queen Sofia Prize for the restoration work done on the complex now housing the Museum of Oaxacan Cultures.

Window of the convent. Protected by a wrought iron grille in the style of the period.

Interior patio. Due to the great dimensions of the convent it has other patios in addition to the main one which were probably used for open air activities such as teaching the catechism.

The architectural features of the convent are similar to those used in Europe in the Middle Ages, and this is expressed in the distribution of spaces in Santo Domingo. The main or processional cloister is outstanding, whose galleries or corridors look onto the central courtyard and the fountain, the symbol of Grace or the Living Stream. The chapter house, the profundis and the refectory are located around the cloisters. Leading to the upper level is a monumental staircase whose lines and

7

Gothic style gallery. *Most galleries in the convent were covered with barrel vaults which show some of the ribs similar to those used in the Gothic style.*

Fresco dating from the 16th century. *Mural painting played an important part the iconography of convents. This fresco shows a member of the Dominican order with two angels.*

Burgoa library. *It bears the name of Brother Francisco de Burgoa who gathered together an enormous number of references about the ways and customs of the Indians of Oaxaca. Created in 1994 with the collection of the Benito Juárez Autonomous University, this library houses more than twenty thousand books ranging from the 14th century to the present.*

Monumental staircase. *Its design and proportions have been compared to those of the one in the monastery of El Escorial, Spain. Its stucco details with gilt applications, together with the richness of its iconography make it a worthy feature of the complex.*

St. John the Evangelist. *Detail of the dome. Depictions of the evangelists are commonly found on pendentives.*

Dome of the room preceding the church. *This is an extraordinary example of molded and gilded stucco. It shows several designs typical of the period around the image of the Virgin who stands on a crescent moon and three angels.*

Entrance to the museum exhibition rooms. *The entrance to the museum, which formerly led to the corridors of cells, is topped by a broken pediment typical of the period done in stucco and gilt. In the center is the coat of arms of the Dominican order.*

Cloister garth. *Surrounded by four corridors with arcades, and in the center a fountain flanked by six columns, the area summarizes the beauty of the complex.*

proportions are similar to those of the staircase in the monastery of El Escorial, Spain.

Another important part of the convent was the garden. Several types of vegetables and fruit were grown there, as well as plants brought from Spain, which the monks took pains to acclimatize.

MUSEUM OF OAXACAN CULTURES

Skull with turquoise incrustations. This is one of the pieces found in Tomb 7 at Monte Albán. Its allusion to death links it with a funeral context at the same time as the stones used to decorate it make it a priceless work of art.

The ex Convent of Santo Domingo de Guzmán has been a museum since 1972. At first it was called the Oaxaca Regional Museum but in 1998 after restoration work had been completed it became the Santo Domingo Cultural Center of Oaxaca. The Museum of Oaxacan Cultures, the Francisco de Burgoa Library, the Botanical Garden, the Nestor Sánchez public newspaper and periodicals library and multi-functional spaces make up this Center. Santo Domingo church, which is open for worship, is administered by Dominican brothers who live there. Divided into fourteen rooms, the museum recreates the history of the state from remote times up to the present day with exhibits of inestimable esthetic value and deep symbolic content. Ranging from ancient cultures to recent finds and restoration work, each of the rooms expresses historical, ideological and artistic changes. In them, several centuries of artistic products reveal the secrets of Oaxaca.

The scribe of Cuilapan. *A figure from Cuilapan, an ancient pre-Hispanic site where today a 16th century convent of the same name stands. It shows a young man seated with crossed legs and his hands on his knees, a common position in pre-Hispanic statues.*

God with a forked tongue. A seated deity wearing a serpent mouth-mask and a conical cap The forked tongue hangs from his open jaws.

Clay box surmounted by a jaguar. Originating from Monte Albán. Made of orange pottery, it was possibly used for ritual purposes.

Room I • Ancient cultures

The different exhibits show the beginnings of the artistic production of the pre-Hispanic cultures that flourished in Oaxaca. Their expressive qualities, iconography, the techniques and materials used, allow us to enter into the thought, ideology and beliefs of these early peoples. The objects on display illustrate the cosmogony, religion and the ideas these ancient cultures had of the world. At the same time they are examples of how these concepts were given physical shape thanks to an extraordinary mastery of techniques and materials, as well as of the language of different genres. They show themes linked to both gods and men, with the natural and the supernatural; tangible evidence of the soul of vanished civilizations.

Anthropomorphic brazier. It depicts the god of Fire The mouth and eyes are cut out. There is a bow shaped motif on the forehead.

Vessel in the shape of a spinal column. The ceramic pieces discovered at Monte Albán included spool shaped vessel supports with paint on clay. Those suggesting a spine are particularly interesting.

Vessel with a double deity. The decoration of pottery with images of gods or animals was common in pre-Hispanic times.

Old man. *This piece illustrates the quality of workmanship in clay for representations of deities or ritual subjects.*

Duality. *Duality governed the thought of ancient Mesoamerican peoples. This piece shows life and death.*

Room II • Times of flourishing

This room shows the heyday of pre-Hispanic cultures in Oaxaca, particularly Monte Albán, from 200 to 900 A. D. —a time corresponding to the Mesoamerican Classic period. This runs from the emergence of the Zapotec culture to the abandonment of Monte Albán, at the time the largest and most important city in the Central Valleys. During this period the cultures consolidated and attained their peak both in religious concepts and artistic expression. Knowledge of astronomy, the

Vessel with monkey. *Anthropomorphic urn depicting the god of Fire. He carries a brazier on his head and is sitting on a Greek fret motif. His features resemble those of a monkey. Made of modeled clay with sgraffito work, it comes from the Cerro de las Minas, Huajuapan de León.*

development of a system of writing, calendars —both the solar one of 365 days and the ritual one of 260 days— and monumental buildings all underline the splendor of this period. An example of this are the exhibits which grace this room, where a visit gives us an idea of the beauty of the arts, the complexity of thought, the mastery and uniqueness of the compositions, their expression and the meaning their shapes hold.

God Pitao Cozobi. Urn with human features and the mask associated with the god Pitao Cozobi. He is wearing a headdress and large ear plugs. He sits cross legged with his hands on his knees, a position common in Mesoamerican art.

Above right, **Opossum.** Opossums appear in various myths in Mesoamerica which show off its distinguishing qualities, in particular its shrewdness.

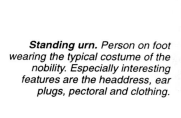

Standing urn. Person on foot wearing the typical costume of the nobility. Especially interesting features are the headdress, ear plugs, pectoral and clothing.

19

Gold mask of the god Xipe Totec. *Xipe Totec was the god of the flayed. With a sacrifice, the victimís skin was removed and placed over the shoulders of the priest, who wore it as a ritual insignia. This ceremony has been linked to agriculture.*

Room III • The treasures of Tomb 7, Monte Albán

Funerary art was undoubtedly one of the most common features in Oaxacan cultures during pre-Hispanic times. Proof of this are the innumerable tombs discovered at Monte Albán, Suchilquitongo, Jaltepetongo, Mitla and other sites. The burial chambers are examples of the plastic integration which dominated the development of pre-Hispanic art. Most of them contain mural painting, reliefs and offerings rich in ceramics and articles crafted in precious metals, such as the case of Tomb 7, to which this room is dedicated. Discovered by Alfonso Caso

Pectoral of Xochipilli. *Xochipilli is considered to be the god of Music and Flowers. He is usually depicted as a young god decorated with flower designs. The piece possibly represents the head of an opossum.*

Pendant with eagle and moon. *This piece demonstrates the quality of workmanship using gold as the raw material. It shows the head of a bird emerging from a sun disk, From the beak hangs a pendant associated with the moon.*

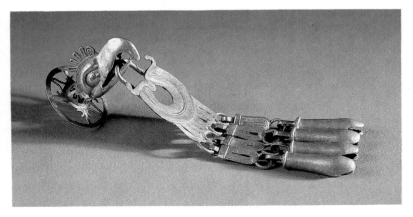

Pectoral of Mictlantecuhtli. *It has been given the name of the god of Death because of the features that look like those of a fleshless person. However, the piece has also been related to the founder of the second dynasty of Tilantongo, based on the dates that appear on the lower sections.*

in 1932, it was constructed by the Zapotecs in the Classic period, possibly to hold the body of a nobleman, judging from its features. The pieces found as part of the offerings included notably numerous objects worked in gold with superb craftsmanship. Goldworking was not a common practice among the other peoples of Mesoamerica so it has great interest, in addition to its esthetic value.

Pendant with falling eagle. *It is associated with the setting sun due to the depiction of a descending eagle framed by a disk. A butterfly hangs from the bird's beak.*

Necklace. *Pendants, pectorals and necklaces deposited in funerary offerings emphasize the rank and importance of the person buried.*

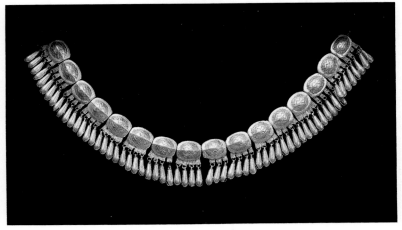

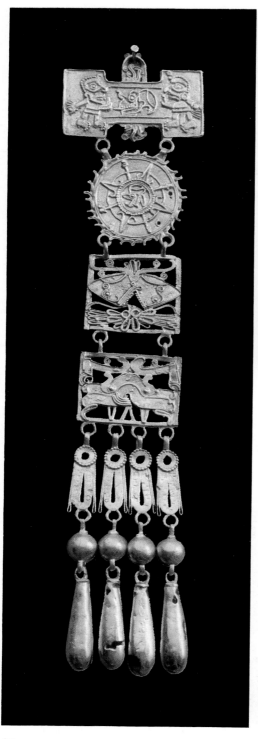

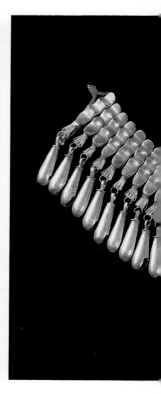

Pectoral. *Pectorals were an essential part of the costume of noble lords. Their features combine esthetic sense with deep symbolic meaning.*

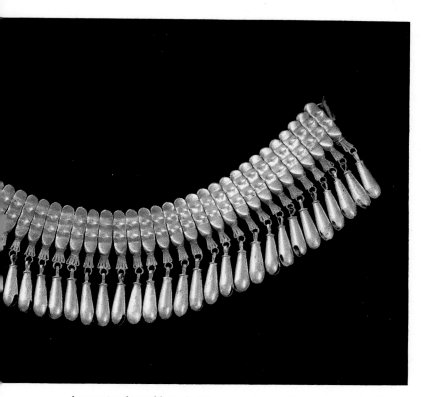

Jaguar teeth necklace. *It was common for nobles to wear animal items as part of their personal adornment. The jaguar was one of the most important deities in the Mesoamerican pantheon.*

Gold feather.
Feathers were extremely important elements in the art of pre-Hispanic peoples. They were part of the headdresses and costume of lords. This piece is possibly an example.

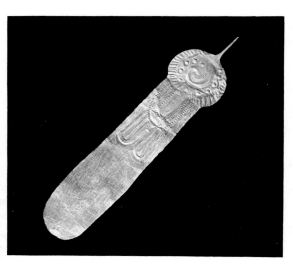

Vessel with opossum's head. *Depiction of animals in funerary vessels was common in Mesoamerica. An example of the custom is this piece showing the heads of two opossums.*

Room IV • The chiefdoms

This room illustrates the post-Classic, from 900 to 1521 A.D., the last of the periods which the history of Mesoamerica before the Conquest is divided into. After Monte Albán was abandoned, other sites arose such as Lambityeco, Mitla and Zaachila in the Central Valleys. The Mixtec occupation of lands where Zapotecs lived previously is the subject of some controversy, but it is believed that in this period, the Mixtec culture was at

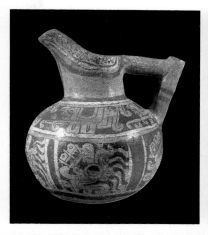
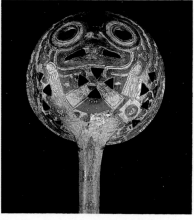

Above left. Polychrome jug. With the polychrome finish typical of post-Classic pottery. It bears different designs, including geometric motifs.

Above right. Censer. Rites and ceremonies were fundamental parts of the duties of men in the pre-Classic era. In them, copal incense played a highly important role This censer was used for burning this aromatic resin used in Mesoamerica.

Below. **Vessel with eagle's head.** A typical ritual vessel found as part of a funeral offering. It represents the body of an eagle.

Vase with hunchback. *People with some kind of physical defect were considered sacred. Representations of hunchbacks are common in Mesoamerican plastic art.*

Censer with woman's head. *Bowl for ritual and funerary use. One of its feet is the body of an anthropomorphic figure, probably a woman. The technique combines cut outs and appliqué.*

its height. Through marriage alliances, the Mixtec domain rose to splendor. With the fall of Monte Albán, Zapotec writing came to an end and there was a surge in the production of codices and codex-like polychrome ceramics, which are exemplified in this room by pieces of high artistic quality whose beauty demonstrates at the same time mastery in the handling of techniques and the perfection of manufacture.

Portrait of Cortés. *The image of Cortés during the Conquest as a soldier and diplomat made him one of the most outstanding figures of the period. In 1529 he was awarded the title of Marquis of the Valley of Oaxaca in reward for his work as a conquistador.*

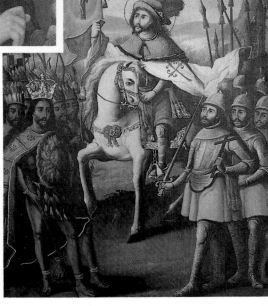

Part of a screen with St. James the Apostle. *This 18th-century painting shows St. James, patron saint of the Conquest. At his sides are some native kings and several conquistadors.*

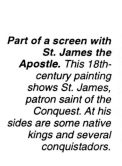

Room V • Contact and Conquest

The second decade of the 16th century tells the story of the Conquest and with it the meeting of two worlds. Europe set its sight on the New Continent and journeyed to it to get to know and transform it. Amid confusion and amazement, the Indians saw how the Spaniards began a process of military, ideological and religious contact. The meeting of different thoughts, languages and customs led to mestizaje, in the co-existence of ways and customs which gradually wove into a complex entity. This room shows the beginning of that process, where conquistadors are the main figures.

29

Room VI • The new faith: writing the past

After the re-conquest of Spain from the hands of the Arabs, there was an emphasis on spreading and promoting Christianity as the only true religion. This is why in New Spain military conquest went hand in hand with spiritual conquest. The brothers who arrived in the new lands brought with them the mission to spread Christianity among the pre-Hispanic civilizations. Their main task was to save the souls of the inhabitants who were ignorant of the true faith. To achieve this, the brothers of the different orders used Indian informants and learned their languages so as to understand the way of thinking of the groups whose souls they wanted to save through evangelization. From this period there are chronicles,

Statue of Santo Domingo. *A wooden statue of whited (estofado) and gilded wood depicting Santo Domingo de Guzmán. The estofado technique consists of applying gold leaf over several coats of whiting which are polished and occasionally painted.*

Friar with informants. *Fragment of a post-Hispanic codex (Yanhuitlán Codex) which shows teaching the Latin alphabet to the sons of Indian nobles. The technique used by the ancient inhabitants of Mesoamerica for their sacred texts continued to be used during the colony as a teaching tool.*

Wooden sculpture.
Image of St. Joachim,
whited and gilded. In
this sculpture the Virgin
Mary's father appears
sitting on a type of
throne.

Double cross. The image of Christ crucified
was not common in the Viceroyalty. The idea
of a bleeding god might appear contradictory
in the eyes of Indian converts to Christianity.
The face of Christ was depicted at the center
of the cross, as in this piece dating from the
18th century.

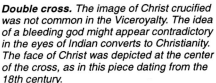

reports and accounts which gather a large amount of infor-
mation about the ways and customs of the inhabitants of these
lands, their ritual practices, their beliefs and the ceremonies
they carried out. Their importance lies in the fact that they are
firsthand sources for interpreting the cultures of the past
through the eyes of the present. These chronicles combine with
the sizeable artistic production characteristic of the 16th century, which includes the construction of large convents, the
creation of reliefs, sculptures and murals. All these were teaching materials which the friars made use of to bring Christianity to the New World.

Metal chest. *Metal objects were manufactured in New Spain with raw material brought from Europe, such as this chest with locks of unusual design.*

Rebozo press. *During the 18th century, rebozos (wraps) were articles of clothing worn by both upper-class women and the most lowly. This exhibit illustrates their importance since technology was used to press them.*

Room VII • The native reply

The three centuries of colonization were distinguished by the ethnic and cultural complexity produced by the mixing of several races. The result of this was the castes which with time and coexistence were enriched and founded part of its life. The assimilation of some elements that were foreign to both natives and Europeans alike was reciprocal. Materials, objects and technologies, as well as institutions and celebrations contributed toward the ethnic and cultural diversity of the Viceroyalty.

Ivory Christ. *Trade with the Orient during the years of the colony. Different raw materials and valuable pieces were obtained by means of the Manila Galleon (Nao de China). An example of them is this 17th-century ivory Christ carved in the Philippines.*

Room VIII • Material and spirit

The baroque took root fruitfully in New Spain. The exhibits in this room demonstrate the New World sense this style acquired during the Conquest. Saints on platforms, altarpieces and painted and gilded figures speak of the religiosity shown through fraternities, patron saints celebrations and guilds. In addition, it is possible to note the taste for materials from other countries, brought by the Manila Galleon (Nao de China), such as the ivories.

Portrait of Benito Juárez. *Benito Juárez played an important part in the history of Mexico. A main player in the Reform he was at the same time the representative of the indigenous class in power when he became president.*

Room IX • Emergence of a new nation

The 19th century opened with the war of Independence. After separation from the Spanish Crown, the new independent nation had to think about its future and identity. It was a century of searches and questioning about the new entity. The decision between a monarchy or a republic, conservatives and liberals, in search of the best proposal to give meaning to the nation. One of the main players in this quest was Benito Juárez, to whom the Reform laws and the separation of Church and State are due. This room is dedicated to him.

Porfirio Díaz, dictator. This picture shows Porfirio Díaz during his exile in France, where he died. He is depicted in full-dress uniform wearing all his decorations.

Porfirio Díaz, general. A Oaxacan commander. As president of Mexico, he showed his interest in making the new nation known to the world.

Room X • Order and progress

Order and progress was the motto of the Porfirian period. The consolidation of Mexico as a nation brought with it the need to show the country to the world. The eagerness of Porfirio Díaz to import European manners and fashions came at the same time as the recognition of the Indian past and its projection outside. The years that the dictatorship lasted were ones of innovations and an effort to provide the nation with the advances of modern times. Mexico shone in the eyes of the world with its entry into the modern age stemming from a revaluation of its past.

Camera and photograph of a Tehuana woman. *From the 19th century, portrais enjoyed great popularity Photography made it possible to capture all the human types and costumes of the period. The old picture shows Doña Juana Cata, believed to have been the mistress of Porfirio Díaz.*

Room XI • Modern Mexico

Technological advances and also the means of communication played a decisive role in Mexico's entry into the modern world. Photography was one of the most used resources in this time of changes and innovations. Thanks to this, pictures still exist that show the subject of this modernity

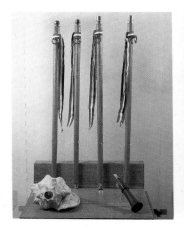

Mayordomo staffs. *Used in Teotitlan del Valle by the municipal president, the supreme authority of the town, or by his assistant the major of staffs. They are also insignia of churchwardens, who are usually elderly men.*

Chinantec huipil (shift). *This garment illustrates the richness of textile making, a legacy from native ancestors. The designs and colors are proof of sensitiveness and a mastery of technique.*

Room XII • Cultural plurality

The ethnic diversity that currently gives life to the polyphony that is Mexico is reflected in the languages, in the eclecticism of customs and traditions, and in the coexistence of all of them.

Room XIII • The defense of memories

The Indian presence in Oaxaca has been a divide in the state's development from a political point of view. But also, and equally importantly, in art. The myths, the colors and sense that keep these people alive can be seen in the plastic arts, in textiles, in music and much else.

Room XIV • Santo Domingo: history and discoveries

During work to remodel the convent, several objects came to light that relate its history, changes and transitions. This room also illustrates the techniques used in the remodeling of the complex, an effort which was rewarded with the Queen Sofia Prize.

Colonial majolica. Pieces discovered during restoration work on the convent of Santo Domingo. The majolica ware produced in the city of Antequera in the second half of the 16th century is an example of a mastery of Spanish techniques that influenced those used in New Spain.

The Botanical Garden. *This is located in the former garden of the convent and contains examples of various species typical of the region.*

The Botanical Garden

This forms part of the Santo Domingo Cultural Center and is located where the garden used to be. Archaeological finds in this area demonstrate its use, since irrigation ditches, drainage channels and some ponds have been discovered, plus other elements which show how important the garden was while the friars were in the convent. Work has been going on since 1998 to develop the Botanical Garden, which is an attempt to show the diversity of the wild plants in Oaxaca's environments, from the wettest to the driest. The Botanical Garden project is an effort to display all this wealth, and also give a new meaning to the space which houses it.

Detail on the facade. *A high relief of Santo Domingo and St, Hippolytus holds up a church.*

The Convent Church of Santo Domingo

Like most 16th century Dominican churches it lies east to west, with the facade in the west. This orientation reveals a symbolic meaning: from the east, where the altar stands comes the sunlight, interpreted as the divine light.

The architectural forms of the building combine features that were in vogue in Europe during the years the construction of it lasted. Thus the facade, built in the 16th century has Renaissance features, while the interior is baroque.

The facade is divided vertically into three sections flanked by two pairs of pilasters. On the horizontal plane there are three sections and a pediment. In the lower section is the great main door flanked by four niches which hold the statues of two Dominican saints, as well as St. Peter and St. Paul.

In the second segment is the dedicatory image of the church. A relief shows St. Hippolytus Martyr who, dressed as an an-

Detail of the family tree. *The ceiling of the lower choir is decorated with the family tree of Santo Domingo de Guzmán in molded, polychrome and gilded stucco. It is one of the finest examples of the art of this period.*

41

Dome of the upper choir. *Worked in plaster and coffering. It consists of ovals containing representations of the martyrs of the Dominican order. The ovals nearest the center contain angels.*

cient Roman, places his hands on Santo Domingo de Guzmán. In the center of the third section is the window of the choir whose stained glass window is modern. The facade is finished off by the figures of the three theological virtues. On the left, Faith is holding a chalice and a cross, Hope carries a balance, and beneath the feet of Charity is the emblem of the Dominican order. Two towers flank the facade.

The interior is built on a cross pattern divided into three main parts: the choir and lower choir, the nave, the transept and presbytery.

Access is through the lower choir covered with a vault which shows the family tree of Santo Domingo de Guzmán in stucco relief. Along the nave are the twelve side chapels dedicated to different saints; on the right side is the remarkable Chapel of

Interior of the church. *The main nave flanked by side chapels has a barrel vault decorated with scenes from the Old and New Testaments.*

Pulpit. *Made of regional woods. The body is decorated with Dominican saints.*

Retable of the high altar. *The original was destroyed by troops who occupied the convent. The present on was built between 1959 and 1961.*

Our Lady of the Rosary, inaugurated on May 5, 1731. Since the Dominicans venerated Our Lady of the Rosary, no expense was spared to build a chapel that would be outstanding for its size and for repeating the shapes of the church, containing as it does choir, nave, transept and presbytery.

Ceiling detail. Most of the decoration of the church was done in stucco and oil paintings, as seen here.

The nave ends in the high altar. It is not the original, since the first was destroyed by the troops which occupied the church. There were several altars until today's was built between 1959 and 1961 under the direction of Father Esteban Arroyo, who took his inspiration from the altar of Yanhuitlán in the High Mixteca.

Virgin of the Rosary. *Flanked by four spiral columns is the image of the Virgin of the Rosary, a Dominican avocation to whom the chapel - the most sumptuous in the church — was dedicated.*

Octagonal dome. *This remarkable octagonal dome shows the evangelists in the pendentives and on the upper part, the apostles. On the keystone is the Holy Virgin.*

Detail of Adam and Eve. Framed by the decoration typical of the church is this picture with a subject from the Old Testament.

Virgin of Guadalupe. One of the various pictures in the church depicts the Virgin of Guadalupe.

Archangel Michael. In this 17th-century painting, the Archangel Michael is shown guiding the celestial armies.

Printed in:
Programas Educativos, S.A. de C.V.
Calz. Chabacano No. 65 Local A
Col. Asturias
06850 - México, D.F. May, 2004
Empresa Certificada por el ISO-9002